Unopened Mail

Unopened Mail

Allan Block
poems 1980-2001

Allan Block

2003

Flatiron Press
Francestown • New Hampshire

Also by the author

In Noah's Wake   1972   William L. Bauhan / Publisher

Allan Block's work has appeared in numerous periodicals and reviews including *The Georgia Review*, *The New Republic*, *The New York Times*, and *The Nation*.

CONTENTS

I

II

III

IV

To Paul Block, who has designed and shaped this book through many technological changes, and has inspired me with his appreciation of poetry; and to Cynthia Gabrielli, poet and translator, whose critiques of my work have graced, guided, and often entertained me.

Our stories are more important than our genes.

– author unknown

part I

Home Remedy

You murder a skunk. At 2 a.m.
in the grass by the overturned garbage can
you waylay him

with a baseball bat. By moonlight,
crooning like a witch, you skin him.
You put him in a pot.

While he simmers you sleep. You dream
of his offended eyes, of how pink he was
without his skin. Meantime

the fat rises in the kettle. The Portugese
woman who gave me this recipe
paused here, forgetting which roots and herbs

her mother added. Was it chicory? Sassafrass?
Anyway, you ladle off the grease,
strain it, bottle it, and drink a dose

for cough. You rub it on your chest for bronchitis.
As a liniment for gout it has
no equal, said Miss DeLuze,

her eyes narrowing. I asked about the smell–
was there any in the meat or oil?
She balked on that detail.

For My Life, Spared

One more down: old classmate Tom,
fattened and killed by his habits.

The hometown weekly I subscribe to
granted him a single paragraph–

birthplace, college, clubs, survivors–
and told nothing of Tom's real wit,

his loud ties and bawling saxophone,
the Honda factory he kept in his bedroom,

the way he sang Aida in falsetto,
how he virtually solved perpetual motion.

Tom and Otto and Eugene and me!
enfants terribles of the Winnebago Valley,

four horsemen of literature and women.
What fine energy we burned! Now

Otto's gone these seven years, and Eugene,
cut down last March in a hunting accident,

leaving me, the frailest of the lot,
my blood thin as vinegar, to puzzle it out

(as though the answer lay in thought).
Tom, old wreck, I sit here chattering!

Lies

Elders, teachers, stuttering children
spoke the truth. I twisted
it for what it could get me.

Cornered by the gang, I
chose their words to fling back at them.
They stuck on them like tar.

Always it worked. Nobody said liar.
They left me alone with my craft.

The Man and Me

He was practical and took over.
Perhaps I was too much of a perfectionist.
I walked around with my head in the planets.

Well, I am calling from Potter's Field
to let me get up, I have good in me.
Give me a chance to benefit the world.

My parents were good people.
I even helped my competitor get started.
Hosannah, it may be too late;

he already has the profit in dollars.
He sits on his terrace overlooking the past,
writing this account. He sits there

like a plumed ape. Do you think he
came to my funeral? He is stupid, and can
write. I am wise and eat mud.

Between the Lions

Once between the lions, the stone lions
on the library steps, he saw strung
gold ropes that reminded him of reins.
Instead of standing aloof and separate
the lions were trying to work together.
It was not a dream: the buses groaned
as they always had; walls of people
lined the great intersection. The lions,
in harness now, acknowledged each other
with a fierce gentleness. If they had wished
they could have moved the whole library
like a wagon down Fifth Avenue.
A poem come quickly on the wings of this.
One writing got it all: it had been dictated.
The poet sat like Leonardo on the curb,
stunned, grateful, staring at his slate.
It was this poem and I am still terrified.

Father, Dying

Always in crowded rooms
somebody is up for death.
Your nostrils will lead you to it.

Father prepared me without lecture.
I smelled it in his scalp where

the hair had gone lame a year before,
and in the clothes he kept

overcolored and spruce. His words,
larded with optimism, spoke more

than any certificate. On his deathbed
he pored over travel atlases.

Rings

(for Barbara)

High lustre, third finger left hand.
Your voice wavers, then instructs:
"The man wears one too." Does he?
I had forgotten. Harnessed, I moan:
"This lock will never yield."

But somewhere I have read:
Prisoners can be released for good behavior.
Long have I served, sullen and soundless.
Spring me, Muse! Give me air, light, song.

You gave me a ring, sweet bride,
The ring of my reluctant voice.
And as we walk, hand in hand, our rings rattle
Like small talk, like silly loops
That clowns invent as they somersault.

4/5/96

Standing

I learned the knack
watching cattle, how they spent
nights sampling grass,

their long torsos parallel,
tails flowing. Where they led me
up slope through juniper,

high in the braided forest
the hemlocks stood on awesome feet.
For half an hour, by moonlight,

backed against a trunk, I must have
dozed upright; I jerked awake,
my spine stiffer than a spike,

then saw the spotted cows again,
downhill and wise, standing
nose by flank; and when

at daybreak they reached the barn,
half-shadow and half-rose with sun,
I watched them slowly file in.

Cloudy Day in the Beehive

It's rotten out. They sit around and bitch
about who'll sweep up, who'll rock the cradle,
who'll make wax. The Queen's a pisser–

foul language in foul weather– she's off her nut.
Entrenched power, that's her trouble–
no man around to cut her down to size.

The drones keep fanning and fussing. You'd think
they'd mutiny or quit, but the system won't let them.
The workers are full of work, but not housework;

see how they loiter and block the exits!
The young in their chambers call for nectar, nectar.
Damn brats! They know instinctively

that history favors those who sit and beg.
The blind rabble climb each other's backs.
They gnash their mandibles. A little sunshine

cutting through would solve it all: silence
the Mad Queen, draw the collectors out,
relax the flowers, elicit that universal

palliative: honey. Or could it be
Brute Nature planned this muddle to remind them
how beautiful it is to fly alone?

Poem

When he pressed his lips to my mouth
the knot fell open of itself.
When he pressed them to my throat
the dress slipped to my feet.
when his lips touched my breast,
everything, I swear
down to his very name,
became so much confused
that I am still,
dear friends,
unable to recount
(as much as I would care to)
what delights
were next bestowed upon me
and by whom.

> after the Indian poet Vikatanamba
> (*translated from the Bengali*
> *by Linda Briggs and Allan Block*)

In the Synagogue

Father and Mother crooned. High in the ark
their covenants lay sheathed in silk.
From hand to hand I passed. The rooms were hot.
I looked and cried. The eternal light went out.

But David's six-pointed, multicolored star
left its brand on me. Walking there
years later, when age had made me clever,
I felt drawn in again, over

my better judgment, to the gloomy place
where minyans were held, and on holy days
old men wailed; where downstairs
the black hymnals lay, where Rabbi Leo Lerner's

yeshiva held me captive, and every timber
exhaled the sweet varnish of piety. Then somewhere
out of history, out of a boy's throat,
(a boy in a yarmulka, pallid and hot)

Kol Nidre, that smitten melody rose,
wavered, and bore against my ears;
and gathering my cooling body and its wit,
I fled for the last time, into daylight.

Birth

The mid-wife said: "That's it."
    She is fat and red.
    She laughs and then she adds:
"Everyone knows what it is."

The mother smiled too.
    She was white as a sheet.
    It's a girl,
One more in the family.

    It's a girl and that's that.

The room smelt of summer,
    Summer with the shutters closed.
    One heard the hay wagons jogging home.
Outside the lizards slept on the stones,

And on the road
    The red hens
    As they rolled in the dust
Cackled like an old man who coughs.

              (from the French of
                C.F. Ramuz)

Jean-David

Yesterday, unknown to you, I saw you walking
through the heavy-scented rose garden,
    absorbed, weary-headed,
    a bit thicker in the waist;

and you were carrying two lives:
    your own, and the one who
    will be born of your sufferings.

Seeing this, I could not check my love.
    What else can I admit?
    Like every idiot with a pen
I'm looking for a touchstone.

And it is you who bids me write.
    When I feel your hand leaning on my arm
and the shadow of your forehead falls
across my cheek,

I seem to be advancing surely with you
towards the realization of a prowess.

                        (from Ramuz)

Stones Unturned

(for Bill Rickenbacker / 1928-1995)

In the dear cornpatch we turned up
Out of hardhack, juniper and briar,
Intrepid boulders crept upward each spring,
Their faces nicked by age and spadeforks.
How far down could their roots extend?
We tried with pries and prayers to unseat them,
But only frost could budge these senators.

Our new-sprung cornstalks never complained.
All three varieties, early, middle, and late,
Took zigzag Indian paths, but always thrived:
Buxom, free of worms, and hugely sweet,
They put the seed catalogues to shame.

Consider the lilies of the field, how they
Sprout and multiply, blossom and wane.
I feel a parallel here: words, too, are kernels
At once amorphous and high-spirited,
Seeking the ultimate sunshine of poetry.
How we toiled and joked over their combinations!
Missing your insights now, I pace the garden
Slowly, more stones than ever underfoot.

Child's Drawing

A road is a crayon line. One bus
humps along it like a caterpillar.
A mountain sharp as an icepick
props up the sun, which ignites
three strenuous sunflowers.
A fish swims uphill. Those
V's trailing after him are not birds,
but his fins, an afterthought.
A small stick figure, triangle for dress,
is signed in fervent yellow: JENNIFER.
Green grass grows
where the paper was too white.

Going Whoring

Undermined by middle age,
rejection slips, a mother's

taunts, the moon out of phase,
no God anyway, and my glut of words

that move nothing, cure nothing,
I go a-whoring for

the anonymous dirty thing
I find draped across bars,

exhaling the gray breath of decay;
and snatching it, call it

courage, redemption, or at
least "provisional love,"

a deceit I can afford at my
age and stage of sophistication

at this time and in this extremity
when all I have is hung.

part II

Unopened Mail

I was all of eleven, a collector of pieces:
broken doll's heads, knives without blades,
expired whistles, rusted dimestore jewelry,
sprung umbrellas. If it was whole
I passed it up. In my resourceful way
I was dean of neighborhood trash.

Today, six decades later, I still hoard.
Now it's unopened mail, addressed
to me or anyone else. The formula is:
scour the streets. No post office monitors this.
Consider it a public service. In cartons
under my bed lie sealed envelopes marked:
URGENT, FRAGILE, ADDRESSEE UNKNOWN,
DECEASED, POSTAGE DUE, INVOICE ENCLOSED.
Savor, comb and caress. Think poetry.

My Cell Mate

He plays his saw. I strum my terrible uke.
Nude, with whoops, we re-enact our crimes.

We break stone in the yard. Our shoulders
touch in recognition. This is for life.

A century passes. We still eat cabbage soup.
We pick each other's fleas. What else?

He is off his mind and looking green.
My thumbs dig in. It is a mercy killing.

Without him no light can penetrate.
The State provides. I am a serial number.

The Poet's Will

It is all words– all artifice.

Who can enforce a poet's last conceit
that leaves his typewriter to X,
his down comforter to Y, his frying pan to Z?

Who can gracefully accept
an expired credit card, a rusted bicycle,
a cracked violin, a wardrobe out of style,
and ten cartons of unfinished manuscripts?

The judge, the court, the attorneys–
each will construe a different document.
Any handwriting expert could declare it
a forgery. It is all

illegal anyway without the official seal
of the Great Probator of Wills
who, even if he issues a final decree,
can never appreciate how

terrified the author was in life
of commas, clauses, codicils, of
a commitment to anything but change;

how determined he was at the end
to cloak himself in metaphor,
to play the consumptive poet
without air, without heirs.

My Cave

It goes way back. Artifacts,
relics of other lives mount in columns,
only a cultivated man can absorb the history.

A single tremulous lantern lights
the etched walls, the jeweled ceilings
hung with daggers. Somewhere a river without source

murmurs its passage. From niches
strewn with ancestors come hollow voices.
I am curator of fossils here, lecturer on lore;

I label mastodon's teeth,
take plaster casts of Mesozoic ferns.
Everything is catalogued and clean. My sign reads:

"Cave of Life. Enter Here.
Witness the Dawn of Creation!
Admission Free." I sit resolutely in the doorway

beckoning, but no tourists come,
no museum directors in black limousines,
no archaeologists wearing their polished hammers.

Probably I ask too much of modern man.
Maybe the location is poor.
I should move the cave to a busy thoroughfare.

Sometimes when I find myself
hemmed in a blind catacomb,
or mired too deeply in dust, I conclude as a scientist

that I am the ultimate fossil,
extinct and gray, my tissue calcified,
cold lime my element; it must be so or I would

have evolved differently: have been
a strong swimmer, say, or have sprouted
wings, a song, fierce pride, and been a soarer.

a dream about audrey

(transcribed intact from a night scribble)

audrey tries to make a
speech/ alas she's drowned out
by the groan of the vacuum cleaner
she has lent me/ this machine
won't pick up dirt/ dirt must be
lifted by hand and fed to the
pipe/ even then it sometimes rejects
it/ it needs oil/ frankly it needs an over
haul/ can't we get a more
efficient cleaner/ either that or
let that girl finish her speech or both/
the point is get rid of the dirt

Two Aunts

1.

Bertha's Kitchen

Pike and whitefish in oval patties,
hot noodle puddings, braided *chollah,*
Napoleon hats of poppyseed and honey;
the high essence of garlic and horse radish,
and in the corner the pickle crock

ripening. I crept here as a boy
under the capacious aprons where
Great Aunt Bertie in a bandana,
honking like a white goose,
ruled her scullery;

and if her secrets were kept
in capped jars, they rubbed off
on me like flour; I am dredged,
I am included in her kneading.
In my sleep I still smell cinnamon.

2.

Like Rebecca

They say I'm like that elderly lady,
impatient, rude, critical.
At the age of 4, stationed at her elbow,
it never occurred to me not to be.

She carried, even in those years,
a peevish, pointed tongue that could fling
gallows humor across the kitchen.
Only now at age 70
does she seem to me
like some ill-natured cocktail hostess,
or, better, like a vaudeville comedienne
going her last round.

Excerpts from an Autobiography

(for Alan Dugan)

I had talent once; where did it go?
planted in the bellies of women;

now have tangible assets: farmhouse,
orchard, pond, potato patch,

children and grandchildren, a book to my name,
a fiddle record, and oh yes,

the leaves of grass in my forehead.
Oh strange chronicles! I remember

each poem and how I surrendered it
unfinished, how I let its lines and pearls

spill out to unsuspecting ladies.
Oh black humor never brought to light!

I walk through my woodlands now,
tongue in cheek, licking my abrasions.

Collected, they make another book.
It is so heavy nobody will buy it.

Peeing Outside

It was, at that age without tools,
the only statement one could make
with one's body, so that
when I chose a geranium
in the rear garden to hose carefully,
and when it shriveled back and stank,
I held myself in terror.

The shock was written on me for years.
I peed away from eyes,
even my own, until
a kind woman, gentler than life,
said, pee here within this tangle,
I like the warmth, I want
just what you make and nothing else.

Thief

For half an hour's skilled labor, his take:
my television, my typewriter, my Hi-Fi,
uncounted records, two watches, a platinum ring,
some pieces of sterling, other trivia.

His residue: a broken window pane,
tobacco shreds, mud from his rippled soles,
the faint odor of shaving soap; no more.
From these traces I reconstruct him:

clearly a man of resource, delicately schooled,
a loner, not a boaster in bars,
driven at times to reckless acts; and if
unwittingly I have described myself, it is

because I've met this petty thief in dreams.
We carry the same satchel, he and I.
He robs the bank, I drive the getaway car.
We laugh and joust, we split our treasure trove.

Living in a Pup Tent

(circa 1929)

Rain or hail on the taut canvas
riveted me to the floor. When snow fell
in the dark I dreamed of white fire.

A cat took refuge there.
I called him Amos– "a mouse",
which was my first outrageous pun.

When crocus appeared outside
my flap door, I cut a bouquet
and tried and tried for scent

until the miracle of lilacs
blew around my corner in May.
A fat towhee cultivated me.

That girl Audrey of bicycle fame
cooked up a storm in me. Compliant I ate
her weed salads and acorn puddings.

Under her gaze I noticed how
rhyme and cadence rose between us
like mushrooms in that humid space,

which would equip me two generations
later to write her, "Little mother,
our kitchen survived the terrible

flood of life...you left your
fuzzy mittens in the cupboard...at long
last I can spell Constantinople."

Snapshots of a Child

One week old and wrinkled he lies,
a grimacing bundle on his mother's knees.

At six months, plump as an ottoman, he
has the eyes of Buddha, the hands of Paganini.

In the bathtub now, he floats a toy;
around his mouth the first lines of irony.

Landed aristocrat, he next surveys
his sandbox estate, his painted cavalry.

Astride a billygoat cart, reins in hand,
he assumes the role of born commander.

Skinny at five, he stands in cowboy hat;
then, dated 1928, comes that harrowing shot

in which, half-stunned and half-amused, he grins
on baby brother with the several chins.

Now boy with collie, boy with garter snake,
with sister Frieda munching birthday cake;

later at 11, young Orpheus, concert star,
he holds the violin that holds his future;

Bar Mitzvah boy, faultless face and clothes;
then class-play Cyrano, banana for nose;

Valedictorian at 17, in cap and gown,
he towers over his Lithuanian cousin;

Taken in marriage at 21, he renounces
all trace of childhood; wedding photos tell

the sudden loss, but can't erase the smile
Satan carved on him, on Satan's child.

Pastoral

That summer of hot days the pond
shrank and shrank. Muck islands rose.
Only the tadpoles could drink such soup.

Long willows dropped confetti.
Frogs from the catacombs spoke
their love songs thick as syrup. It was then,

out of the August cauldron,
the cicada began his difficult lyric,
a note like gravel, rising

until the hemlocks shook. It woke even
the rain which broke in such baritone
I ran to save my skin. Storing

heat I let water bead on me and
pop dry. My whiskers curled tendrils;
Reborn at fifty, I bleated like a kid.

My Defects

My nostrils are not beautiful.
    I stoop. I'm wafer thin,
    hairless as a melon.
Blue tributaries clasp my legs.

I lack compassion, I pollute,
    covet money, procrastinate,
can't organize a day's work.

I am possessed of
    short vision
    short memory
    short wind
and a shorted heart that murmurs its revenge.

There are blemishes on me
nobody has yet identified:
    a streak of sadism
that wants others to squirm;
    a tendency to offer
affection and then retract;
my inability to share my sleep with anyone.

Food is my ranking passion.
    The image of myself
    I hold most dear
is a figure Bosch might have painted
    of a sitting troll
    stuffing his hollow
with rich delicatessen
    while on a branch nearby
    a lone nightingale weeps.

Quintuplet

Two girls. A third. A fourth. And now
this last fetus, all male, scratches its dome,
yawping to be out.

It has been a hard life
in a pressure cabin, treading water.
Hey, gargoyle!

this is a crowded highway.
The trick is not to push, but to
hang onto a rafter

gathering breath; and when at last
you appear, livid
from having been outscored by women,

the world will have a name ready for you:
Vincenzo the Magnificent,
the Red Pepper with Hands.

The Apple Pruner

In February's hard light
my hundred decisions rebuke me.
The ground boils with branches.

No surgeon can understand
how many apples I have stolen;
and it is painless, perfectly painless.

After His Death

(3 attempts at an epitaph)

A tape of the poet's voice has been unearthed.
At one point he talks with fervor and regret
of his output, the few flawed volumes he left behind.
"Literature will be the weaker for me," he laments.

In another section he explains frankly
what he meant by poetry, what he intended
in his most obscure poems: "I owe this to the world.
Now that you know, don't bother to read me."

Reversing his position toward the end,
he exalts himself, at the same time remaining loyal
to his injured pride; and here the tape runs out:
"It takes a great mind to obliterate itself."

The Word Love

I would like to find a use for it
beyond the statement of the thought
it passes for; for instance,
if a tree could be named for it, the tree
might spiral upward in an unspoken
movement of its veins and pulp.
If a boat were named for it, the boat might
run in unison with the waves,
perfectly oarless and motorless;
and if a man could know it
as something besides a sound,
an easy syllable fitted to his tongue,
he might, touching it, feel it slip altogether,
but at least
his love would be lived and not called.

The Suitors

These are the suitors holding fresh bouquets
Who come like tired lawyers to a case,
With frayed portfolios and an old refrain.
They are not suitors waiting to be felled
By some enraged Ulysses ploughing home;
One titter of approval nourishes them,
One bold stroke of carrom or deuces wild
And to all watchers they are reconciled.

They press the bell; within the matron pouts,
Playing among her careful scents and lamps.
She descends all vibrant; then begins the bout,
The slow jockey for position as each encamps
Upon her fringe, but when she wheels away
She scatters all their brilliant white bouquets.

part III

Feeding the Pelicans
(Captiva, Florida)

That day, it seems a century ago,
last winter, when the pelicans
sat resolutely, like Roman senators,
one on every post, watching us
fish until we had a dozen or so
small whitebait all gathered in
a plastic pail, one large bird,
older and craftier than the rest,
his cheeks all frizzed with white hairs,
came gliding down to where we sat.
The sight of our silver minnows
sent him into a shivering ecstasy.
He would have scissored them right
out of our hands into his canvas bill
had we not shooed him off a few feet
to make room for the other hungry birds.
We tried feeding them all equally,
giving the shyest a bonus for being shy,
but the crafty one, the glutton, speared
an extra portion by sheer bravado.
That day last winter, like ten-thousand
other days, has lost its identity,
but I can't forget the foremost pelican,
the way he dropped his potato-sack
bulk at our feet, how he riveted us
with a lemon-yellow eye that said
he was worth an extra morsel, surely,
for being such a perfect bully,
for being half-bird, half-reptile,
the last living pterodactyl.

Catalpa

Freakish, bare
too much of the year,
big limp leaves pinned on
ungainly skeleton,
nightmarish blossoms,
pods as long as snakes;

all pith, shallow root,
joints brittle, chemistry dull,
no poise, no mettle,
heart rotted out,
snaps in the wind.

Echo

The valley where I go to test my echo
Is full of distractions: the bluejay's talk,
The hare's stacatto thump, the beetle's click;
At night the chorus of frogs; and the wind itself,
Unanswerable! Where can I go
In this rabid auditorium to find
A clear report, an echo of my own?

Now at the valley's highest ledge I
Shout across its lap of foliage
With a mock exasperation.
My cry bounces back sharply, then rattles on
Like tissue paper blown against a screen.
But the measureable fact remains:
I echo, therefore I am.
It is not only doubt that preserves me.

Reflections

It is hard for a poet to look in the mirror.
He sees the craters of his eyes,
his mouth stitched like a baseball,
the stone outcrop of his nose; he sees

flickering across it all
the badge his tribe left on him:
a smile neither of amusement nor satisfaction.
Ah, if only his tribe could be located

a map might be provided of hills,
peaks, caves with scrolls hidden in them.
But his tribe is lost twelve times over.
His languages are lost or siphoned off;

he must pick new words from the dust.
The mirror honeycombs his face
in cross-section like a glass ant-colony.
Among the tunnels, the filigree

of aisles, there are no trophies left.
They have been picked clean by the collectors.
His face has been ravished of its lines.
He stands tethered to a smile.

Three Memos to my Secretary

9 a.m.

I enter my translucent office,
still dreaming of how
all last night I held you in my crescent,
cupping your forehead in sleep.

But your body, its sheer forehead,
Its triggered limbs, is already
beyond reach, its fingers stroking
not my vulnerable loins
but electric keys, my crash of words.

12 noon

Oh, we tried it a lot of ways:
on your desk, in my swivel chair,
on the pea-green carpet, or standing up

in the elevator, clenched like clams.
During coffee break we did
lascivious things with our eyes

while the percolator wolf-whistled.
All morning we played yin and yang,
but the glass partitions mocked us,

the fluorescent lights stared us down.
We were trampled into the rug
by the heels of business. Here at midday,

herded by hunger, we mount
the sandwich counter in a last attempt
at perfect unity, a work of art.

5 p.m.

Dear Daylight Priestess, your hair
in tangles, wearing a halo of ink–

here at the close of business, at sundown,
let us worship, formally,

in the lotus position, breathing deeply,
the Great Cause we both labor for,

its pristine light and logic, that we may
by sheerest concentration, understand

what keeps us here, why for this concern we
lose time and ink and hair and dignity.

For Arthur S. Who Moved to the Country

A beautiful exit he made of it–
    no fanfare, no idle talk, you <u>felt</u> the integrity.

    And now–
    these dull routines:
    patches to be sewn,
    chinks to fill,
    meat to be coaxed to his pot,
    the eternal fire to feed.
    Each morning he has
    the same quarrel with mute nature
    he had with the world of noise
    before he bolted it.

    Friend, take heart!
    the soot is still flying
    on your old ledge.
    Your engines, your sculptures,
    nobody can move them!

Chatterly: an Epigram

They spoke little. The man did
what he had to do, as though it
were plowing, harrowing, transplanting,
then returned to his greenhouse, she to
her guests, straightening herself, talking
calmly of foxes, lady's slippers, quail
lately come to her meadows. The summer wore on;
she took her daily walk around the farm,
stopping at his cabin; bore his weight
as one might endure another social call,
without belief; and in the end
saw, running the whole machine,
that important cog, her husband, for
the clean, comfortable burden he really was.

Impresario

Looking at his rotogravure likeness,
Confident, quick, flamboyant,
By what chemistry did I see instead
A 12-point caribou, taken at gunpoint,
Not a hair missing, a museum specimen,
Good face, good figure, white teeth, glass eyes?

The Flying Carpet

Good at last to travel
nowhere and meet the clouds
slanting in silence

through wind tunnels, to feel
the sun in its domain,
to be borne where weather is born;

good to be where each breath
we draw is like the first
cool jet of sustenance

between our gums and in our lungs;
good to have the air so thin,
and so little to fall back on

of what we were below;
good also to reflect
how much we tried and never tested,

and how much of what we actually did
on ground level was unsound;
good to acknowledge

we're on this rug together
without map or compass or power
or even the power to collapse,

and where looking outward
over the fringe, we confront
areas so familiar we wallow

in them like the mothering
water so salted to the taste
which wafted us once

weightless and white like this,
our lips churning bubbles,
our large eyes seeking a shelf.

Overweight

Fat girl! Bessie Garby! in our small town
you were the nearest we had to a sideshow.
Curlers in your hair, you'd wade
up Main Street, between strawberry sundaes,
big as a billboard in your flowered skirt.

You knew what the public wanted. Sundays
they'd elevate you on an ice cream stool
under a parasol. The bravest stayed to chat.
Your raw, contralto voice boomed through the park,
"You bet! You bet!" It was disease you spoke about,

phlebitis, gout, a balm for your fallen arches.
We children squirmed. We wanted you tattooed.
"Fat Garby!" we'd shout, then dive for shrubbery.
We ravished you for a decade, until you became
routine as traffic, thinned by overuse.

Land Mine

That chemical bomb I manufactured,
planted and forgot so long ago
lay breathing half a century. The day

my toe triggered it by mistake
the earth rose in a geyser.
I thought my head vaporized.

In the sick vacuum that followed
I stood without camouflage,
my feet among coals, and wept

for the booby trap I'd set myself,
for my overwrought modern skin;
and as the air cleared of ash

and sun and shadow reappeared–
limping, I felt sweep across my brow
the pure wind of accident.

For Two

I've set the table for two; you arrive
Wearing my conciliatory orchid.
Our bill of fare: to sit and chat,
To dine wisely and forego history,
To seal it with a toast.
This truce, one feels, will last and last.

The table, fresh as an island, offers
Roast and wine, the proper herbs,
No awkward sentiments, no loose ends,
And the assurance of having things
Continued under oath:
Good wine, a friend, a fire in the hearth.

I touch my guitar. What I have to play
Is incidental music, but I try.
You laugh a little; the mood is set,
Not overstated, and after that
Another nightcap says it's
Getting late and we must go our ways.

You slip out gracefully. I latch the door,
Knowing the pact final, inked and dried.
Inward again, I stumble past the white
Innocuous table where lie strewn
My tenderest illusions,
The best of my tricks, the wildest of my passions.

Road

It led, said the map, from X and Y,
anonymous red dots, to Z, famous for embroidery,
an hour's drive away.

Seated behind glass, folded like maps,
we rode, in fact, the tenuous line
marked highway; but even then,
before we could acknowledge it as concrete,
the 40-odd miles to Z had surrendered
to our prepared reflexes. We found
no needlework, no museum, and as
we hairpinned backward for the ride to X,
turning, we learned
to fit the road to the abstraction,
the abstraction to the road.

Rhode Island Boulders

These terra cotta granite slabs
shaped like animals, that stud the coastline
near Sakonnet Point, excite and trouble me.

The water swelling around them
makes them appear to rise and fall–
peach-colored whales and mastodons
out sunning, gulls perched on them,
barnacles crusting their sides. I could
accept them as fully alive, only
memory pinches: I had an agate once,
same salmon pink, same opaque density,
my father'd given me out of

his collection of stones, antique glass,
and Ford Model-A gearshift handles.
It bristled with luck, but one winter day,

while rolling it on the carpet indoors,
I saw it disappear down a hot air register.
My luck sank with it, like so much

provisional joy I've felt, and felt escape;
and though I keep a marble with me always,
my fortunes, here and now, run average.

A Recurrent Dream

Each night I am freshly in it,
the dream of chronic backsliding.
It is classic now: me in my '58 Dodge,
hurtling through traffic in reverse
like some fool antic of the Keystone Kops.
Backwards, faster and faster,
pumping the brake for dear life, I careen
through intersections, past red lights,
past the flood of pedestrians.
Always it is close, nobody injured,
the car intact, its gears
miraculously unstripped: but I wake up
with a Charley Horse leg,
a kink in my neck from craning.

Some night I will clamp a lid on it,
label it "Obsolete" and file it away,
and that will end the series,
but not the peril. The peril that brings it on
is endemic. Each day supplies it
with the nerve to go back to it.
Each night frays those nerves, saying:
"Eyes front. Deep breath. Ride it out."

On a Bird, Waking to Snow

The afternoon before the night he
Went to sleep, the sky had been
Grey powder rammed together. Then he forgot.
His belly full, his legs vaguely sore
From foraging, he blew himself
Into the wind-resistant ball
He needed to be for the night, buried
His head against noise, and slept
The sleep of the dead until he woke.

And his waking was sudden. A cold weight
Lay on his shoulder. His wide eyes
Dwindled to points as he sprang
Sidelong into glare. Oh he was awake!
The sky, a wall of grains, bore down on him.
The bushes, from above,
Were rounded forms he could not fasten on.
A great land rose under him like fur.
He would fly down and meet it;
He would have to stand on it, or starve.

Intangibles

The swallow's preference for barns,
white light divided in a prism,
creation's instant, the pointed tongues
of flame between logs, distances,
curved frequencies of tides, lunar
phases, formulae, phyla, valences,
the mouse's hunger pangs, buried
treasure and its tales, the blue of
icicles, evergreens' blue-green,
the head my father carried to his grave,
bear stars and porpoise galaxies,
chiaroscuro, gender, logic
and its failure to convince, herds,
absolute zero, blood ties,
these lines I address to your face,
whales' cemeteries, centaurs' stables,
allegiance to flags, my interest
in scatology, a tally of sand grains,
round numbers, cube roots,
the seventeenth year of the locust,
firefly fuel, our fall from grace,
and many others; also the blush I blush
lest something be too tactile in these forms
by definition lonely to the touch.

A Dream of Hands

Floundering again in dreams,
    I offer you something of my hands:
a pair of canvas gloves I wore

for gardening and let mildew. Here, take them,
    treasure them, they contain
all the fondling potatoes crave,

enough finesse to shape a perfect rose.
    Keep and explore their lucky fingers. But now
your hands, far from accepting mine,

break out in warts, in rabid fungus.
    I rack my brain for remedies, while
you press your afflicted hands between

the pages of a dictionary, which in turn
    grows lobes like a giant lung,
like a mushroom that knows no boundaries.

Husband

She marveled at all that went through him:
the beer, the baseball, the dime
novels, racing sheets, pretzels– everything
ravished and tossed in the corner in the
crass male way. Shoved against her,
how well the bully slept!
Awake and watching, she felt her flesh
crawl; and marveled and felt married
to him and his litter,
and forgot Christ, and parted her legs
for more of him, her bullpricked
Billy the Kid third baseman.

part IV

The Devil's Heir

The Devil, after years
in office, rears
a brood of average children
who in time learn
their father's occupation.
Horrified but entranced, they turn
their confusion into games
that kill for glee. At times
they dabble in black magic. On
learning they have cloven
hoofs and incipient horns and tails
like their father, the little angels
run amok, stealing and laying waste
like young Trojans. Eventually they adjust
except for one freckled brat
who sneaks off to a friend's flat
to mix explosives. Next morning
at breakfast he denies everything.
Behind his newspaper the Devil
goes rigid, but manages a smile
at the turn of events. Young Lucifer
slouches. He feels his brows catch fire;
and suddenly, spooning his oatmeal,
the new heir shrugs and makes it real.

In a Dory, Crossing the Atlantic

It is not your palms and shoulders, but
your eyes that chafe from the
exercise of encountering nothing.

One way to save your eyes is to
run them critically along the gunnels.
Notice the wide belly for less roll,

the high prow for splitting waves, and the long
spine for bridging them, and you will
know how unsinkable you are, how

the world is pulling for you to pull
through the Azores to Portugal,
in your one-man shell, your one-man ocean.

The Broken Crutch

I found an old crutch on the beach.
I leaned on it and it felt good.
But what was its meaning?
Was an old man washed out to sea?
Had someone very old, on a ferry boat, fallen overboard?
Was this crutch a warning to me
    not to venture too far into the surf
    or too near the big boulders against which
    the big waves crashed?

I tend to take things seriously.
Omens lead my life.
I feel a crick in my joints and I go to bed.
I think I hear the waves speaking
    and at once it is an ominous message
    intended for me alone.

But today, riding a wave of boisterous life
and against my better judgment,
    I did 40 pushups on the beach
    while a family of white swans
    looked on impassively.
I thought that a good omen, a kind of blessing.

The Symphony Conductor

You glance at the other stallions
at work beside you, tossing their pompadours
toward the ladies, and you decide

any hundred mounts can make music, given
the fanfare, the stadium, the paying public.
So you reach out, you stroke more brilliantly.

The herd leaps. Now at the final chord
real thunder breaks from the stands.
The air is filled with roses and handkerchiefs.

You launch three encores. Then suddenly
there is no soloist like yourself, no ensemble
can contain you, and you bolt,

stampeding up the aisle, past garlands,
past the rung syllables of your name,
through lobbies, under billboards advertising

your career, into the common boulevard where
among hoot and crash, siren and catcall,
all sound and the memory of sound vanish, so that

as you gasp, there begins behind your ears
the whisper of death and you are
at last a hollow reed, a string, an echo chamber.

Detour

When we came to the turn, we took it,
Leaning inward, buckled to our cushions,
As though the road could spiral off the map.
Not that it hairpinned backward, ever,
Or knotted itself in a cloverleaf; but maps
Can falsify, compasses can wander.

The map failed, we thought. Its blues, blacks,
Reds and greens piled up before our eyes
Like warnings. In turn we betrayed the map
By lack of belief. So when the highway
Failed to cut a path to common sense,
We felt the journey slip through our fingers;

And though our fingers often traced
The printed pattern of that journey,
Alert to every contour, line, and symbol,
We could never pinpoint the genesis of error.
It was only in motion that we learned
No road can take us where we want to go.

Wallflowers

I wish I
could let them be the
coy, anemic, sedentary roses
some 19th century farmer's wife
glued to her bedroom walls to give her
the illusion of summer during her white, prosaic winters.
But I have looked at them too long and too intensely.
All day, printed inside my eyelids, they
race up, down, across, diagonally,
like molecules or words, shaking
out of the flat, toward
a new synthesis.

The Violet

I rose in April; the hedge was low,
The buds were nearly open. You rose too.
You were Midget, who lived across the road.
I was Blackjack, and I had no God.
Disguised, grim, each with his satchel,
We crossed the orchard, scaled the wall,
Hard for felony that day, until
Cool in the patterned silence, there it was,
Protruding from its mother moss–
The violet we transplanted in the fall,
The one we'd pressed against the wall,
Out of the weather, and then forgot.
Beside the slender stalk we knelt,
Awed by the purple cup and throat,
The downward face, the obstinate root.
Was it a trick of climate that gave it
Prodigious life, but sapped us white,
Turning our assassin's nerves to jelly?
You said, "Let's pick it!" and looked silly
As you cursed, spat, and kicked the ground.
Lifting our burglar's bags, we slunk around
To Paine's Hollow where we unwound
Our hangman's noose, delved under rock,
Explored the edges of a lake,
Poked up a wad of burrs that stuck,
But failed to find another victim.
When dark and hunger drove us home,
You down your path, I toward mine,
Your face grew lank again, withdrawn,
As though you were the hunted one.
We parted, lootless still, and yet
I knew no color deep as violet.

Winter Bird

Peering down aisles of snow
The pigeon on the stone cornice
Situates himself for winter.
An astute bird, a sentinel
Who pivots on high masonry
As though to catch and diagram
The weather annals of our city,

He eases along his chimney ledge
In harmony with air and morning bells,
While trucks and men below
Toil in the heavy drifts.
At length he flutters to the sill
In a shower of dry snowflakes
To prey on our good nature.

Our crumbs, our wilted salads
Contain his necessary spark.
In return be bestows no song,
No show of gaudy feathers,
But only his drab, repetitive
Throaty cooing, like the hum
Of radios in distant rooms.

To think of his life blood,
Caustic and thin as iodine,
Warming his fragile legs,
Is to perceive him accurately,
A gray bird in a winter setting,
Vicar in a belfry, needing
Sometimes bread, never pity.

The Heretics

For centuries they languished in a tent
From dawn until the setting sun, and stared
Upon vague trees sunk down in excrement,
Or bellowed in the dim and freezing air.
Some carried their affliction like a stone
Worn round the neck. The others sought a place
Within some cave where they might sigh and drone
Unrecognized by any human face.

One day a splendid stranger came, full
Of a transient grace, and leaned against the wall,
And calling each by name, stroked every head
Until they raised up and were comforted,
And all of them began to say and do
The things that they had always wanted to.

Kilroy

WAS HERE, is gone,
leaving his scrawl
in every cubicle
(find one
he hasn't loitered in).
We who follow
breathe his acrid air
gratefully, like disciples,
filling his absence
with no common flesh (let the God be)
until we see
emblazoned in Delaware
the gross news:
KILROY AND MARY WERE HERE.

The Married Couple

They took an innocent day
full of the meekest shadows, and by
insult and counter-insult, sickened it
until the air was black with malice.

If there could be fulfillment in malice
they achieved it. Back to back, their eyes
at furthest compass points, they savored
each innuendo like a happy meal.

But then, belching and spattering,
A real catastrophe rained down on them.
Hot ashes settled in the patio.
Lava crept across the tiles

where their toes were, and by degrees,
first reflexively, then with calculated lust,
lurching forward in the holocaust,
they clasped each other and were fused,

while around them, unnoticed, columns fell,
cats fried, wine bubbled off,
the state and its archives withered away,
and gulls collided, barking at the sky.

Cornucopia

The man at the sandwich counter
sat exploring. Besides pastrami,
a voyage in itself, there was the weather,
the presidency, and yesterday's grand larceny.
He gave his considered views,
and I, dribbling mayonnaise,
could see only his gold teeth, his florid
nose tip. I knew
from his reservoir would come
only the direst predictions,
but I liked the way the
pumpernickel disappeared,
the smack of meat and mustard,
the chef grinding at his job,
and the passionless face
of the clock overhead.

A Boy and a Bushel of Apples

For once, let him sample every one,
Let him puncture, split and scar
With his unbridled, curious teeth
And sooty fingers, each perfect globe.
Give him entire this October basket
To wallow in, as though it were
Pandora's box of baubles, and let him
Stamp his impish imprint on each, a coy
Bird-beak nip, a thumbnail scratch,
Or total obliteration. If these

Dozens are not for him, then for whom?
Not for the feckless farmer
Who sells them off before they're ripe,
Nor for the housewife, in whose picture
Window they languish in a bowl.
They belong to all hasty devourers:
Jet-winged blackbirds, intoxicated mice,
The midnight otter, the provident squirrel;
To pairs of parallel horses; also to
The slow consumers: grub, mildew, frost;

But mostly to boys, the brawny, the bold,
The pasty and the pink, the early riser,
The canny liar, the lopsided walker,
The bluff, the brainy, the unhappy bully,
The true trout-fisher, the mother's treasure...
If there is one who typifies them all,
Single him, brawling, from the rest, and
Planting him under the spell of harvest,
Just once, without regret, grant him
All the apples he can eat or break.

For Paul

The Swelling Under the Waves

The river dips widely from the source,
The sand clings to the shore.
A girl swims through broken light
Amid the fast water's roar.

She circles in the gathering wave
Or rides the top of foam
Till, caught in the heavier breakers,
She gives over her form.

Where the river slows and widens
Among flat gleaming beds,
She tires of all but the silence
And a white cloudiness overhead.

Where river and sea meet, she sets
An ancient boat adrift;
With no more sound than the current
She handles the turning raft.

Past moons cold as the night
She dips and softly steers
Into the swelling under the waves
Toward a love that never moves.

*This book
was composed and printed
in Century Schoolbook with
headings in Century Schoolbook Bold at
Wallace Press / Reprographics in Concord, New Hampshire
and bound at the New Hampshire Bindery
Concord, New Hampshire*